Native American GAMES and Stories

James Bruchac and Joseph Bruchac
Illustrations by Kayeri Akweks

fulcrum resources
golden, colorado

Library of Congress Cataloging-in-Publication Data

Bruchac, James.
    Native American games and stories / James Bruchac and Joseph Bruchac ; illustrated by Kayeri Akwek.
        p. cm.
    Includes bibliographical references and index.
    ISBN 1-55591-979-0 (pbk.)
    1. Indians of North America—Games—Juvenile literature. 2. Indians of North America—Social life and customs—Juvenile literature. [1. Indians of North America—Games. 2. Indians of North America—Folklore. 3. Folklore—North America.] I. Bruchac, Joseph, 1942– II. Akweks, Kayeri, ill. III. Title.
    E98.G2 B78 2000
    796'.089'97—dc21

                                                                00-010016

Printed in Canada
0 9 8 7 6 5 4 3

Fulcrum Publishing
16100 Table Mountain Parkway, Suite 300
Golden, Colorado 80403
(800) 992-2908 • (303) 277-1623
www.fulcrum-resources.com

To Ryan and Warren—whose hearts are in the game.

One widespread American Indian belief is that you can learn while you play and play while you learn. The aim of this volume is to share—with parents, educators, and kids—some of those stories and related activities that are great for both teaching and fun.

Acknowledgments

We owe a special thanks to our good friend and teacher, John Stokes, who has spent many years sharing these old skills with both young and old through The Tracking Project. Our own Ndakinna Wilderness Project is an outgrowth of the good work John Stokes has continued to do with Native and non-Native people in many parts of the world.

Contents

Ball Games
and
Team Sports

Everyone Is
Part of the Team:
Native American Team Sports

The idea of team sports appears to have been more common among American Indian peoples than anywhere else in the world. Although it is hard to believe today, such popular team sports as basketball, soccer, hockey, football, and baseball were all invented within the last two hundred years. They seem to have been based more on American Indian ideas and games than anything else.

Of course, there were spectator sports in Europe and Asia before Europeans first made contact with this continent. But the games and sports of Europe and Asia were quite different. Races on foot, on horseback, or in chariots, as well as, wrestling, boxing, and archery, were very popular.

This is the Choctaw form of lacrosse, called "stickball" by the Southeastern Choctaws. The sticks are made out of hickory wood and are about three feet long.

But games that involved two teams, aside from such things as the tug-of-war, were rare. Most games were individual contests, with one person or another winning. And ball games with two teams really did not exist in Europe before the fifteenth century. In Asia, such sports as polo, which involved teams on horseback striking a ball with a mallet, did exist. But they were not played by many people. In Europe and Asia in the centuries before America was "discovered," there was little time for playing. Life was too hard for the majority of the people. Playing games was not a big part of everyday life for European or Asian people in those days. Only the wealthy and powerful had time to play.

But in Native North America, playing games was an important part of everyday life for everyone. Games taught people how to cooperate. Team games were a way of bringing people together and reminding people to include each other in their activities. They strengthened people's bodies and minds. Whether you were male or female, young or old, you could take part in team sports in virtually every Native American tribal nation. Even old people who had to lean on a stick to walk would join in the game. Sometimes, there would be ball games that pitted all of the people of one village against all of the people in another village with the goals set miles apart! One French visitor to North America described seeing the Huron people playing a game of lacrosse in which hundreds of players took part. Team sports were so important that the birds and animals, and even the thunder beings that lived in the sky, were said to enjoy playing ball games.

What kinds of ball games did Native Americans play before the coming of Europeans? If we look to the writings of early European visitors to North American and Central America we may be surprised at just how widespread and various the ball games were. Generally, in the area now known as the United States, the pre-Columbian Native American ball games can be divided into four kinds: racquetball (like lacrosse) and doubleball (in which one or two sticks take the place of the racket and the object caught and thrown consists of two balls or sticks sewn or tied together); football (like soccer); shinny (like ice or field hockey); and ball races in which a ball or another object is kicked along a course by two or more players racing each other.

Perhaps the first Native American ball games to be described were those of the area we now call New England. In the early 1600s, a man named William Wood observed the Massachusets playing a game that he called "football," in which two opposing teams tried to score goals by kicking a round ball with their feet on a flat sandy field a mile in length (*New England's Prospect,* London, University of Massachusets, 1477). In 1643, Roger Williams described the way the Narragansett people of Rhode Island played their version of football, *pasuckquakowauog,* or "town against town" (*Key into the Language of America,* London, Gregory Dexter, 1643).

In 1703, Baron La Hontan gave a description of the game of racquetball as it was played by the Hurons of eastern Canada. "They … play with a ball not unlike our tennis, but the balls are very large, and the rackets resemble ours, save that the handle is at least three feet long. The savages, who commonly play in large companies of 300 to 400 hundred at a time, fix sticks at 500 to 600 paces distant from each other. They divide into two equal parties and toss up the ball about halfway between the two sticks. Each party endeavors to toss the ball to their side…. All these games are made only for feasts or other trifling entertainment; for 'tis to be observed that they hate money, so they never put it in their balance" (*New Voyages to North America,* Volume 2, London, H. Bonwicke et. al, 1703).

In the racquetball games widespread among all the Native peoples of the northeast, a single netted stick was used to catch and throw a small ball toward the goal. In 1809, Alexander Henry described the game as it was played among the Michigan Chippewa. "Baggatiway, called by the Canadians *le jeu de la crosse,* is played with a bat and ball. The bat is about four feet in length, and terminating in a sort of racket. Two posts are placed in the ground, at a considerable distance from each other, a mile or more. Each party has its own post and the game consists in throwing the ball up to the post of the adversary" (*Travels and Adventures in Canada,* New York, I. Ripley, 1809). Mrs. W. W. Brown wrote about the game as it was played by the Passamaquoddy of Eastport, Maine, in the late 1800s. "E-bes-qua-mo'gan, or game of ball, seems to have been the most popular and universal of the outdoor games.... Tradition gives it a prominent place in their wonderful mythology. The Aurora Borealis is supposed to be Wa-ba-banal playing ball. Among the Wabanaki it was played by women as well as men" ("Some Indoor and Outdoor Games of the Wabanaki Indians," *Proceedings and Transactions.* Ottawa: Royal Society of Canada, Sec. 2, No. 6, 1888, 41–46). Brown also described the goals in the Wabanaki game not as posts, but as two holes dug into the ground.

Among the Cherokees and other tribes of the southeast, two rackets with smaller webbing were used. The Eastern Cherokees called the game *anetsa,* and its play was so important that numerous ceremonial preparations were undertaken by the players before each game. Ball players trained rigorously and special dances took place before the games were played. A long and wonderfully detailed description of everything done before, during, and after a Cherokee ball game was written by James Mooney in 1890 after watching a game played by the Eastern Cherokees in North Carolina ("The Cherokee Ball Play," *The American Anthropologist 3,* 1890: 105–132). A small wooden ball or a buckskin bag stuffed with deerhair was commonly used. Racquetball games were mostly found in the northeast and the southeast along the Atlantic coast, through the Great Lakes region, and into the eastern plains.

Shinny, in which a ball is struck by a stick and driven toward a goal across either the ground or the frozen surface of a pond, was so widespread across North America that Stewart Culin called it "practically universal among the tribes" ("Games of the North Amer-

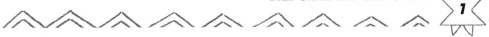

ican Indians," *Twenty-eighth Annual Report for the Bureau of American Ethnology.* Washington D.C.: Government Printing Office, 1911, 37–819). The Arapahos called this game *gugawhat,* playing it with a buckskin ball filled with buffalo hair. On the Pacific coast, where the Wasama people of Madera County called it *mula,* the ball was made of a wood knot from the mountain mahogany tree. In the northwest, the Makah people played the game after killing a whale, carving the ball from a soft piece of whalebone. In the southwest, among the Navajos, it is called *ndashdilka'l* and a bag-shaped ball is used. The goals might be a single post or two posts at each end of the field, a line drawn on the ground, or even two blankets spread out side by side. Sometimes men and woman played apart and sometimes they played against each other. The rules of these various games in which the ball was struck by a bat or a curved stick varied greatly. In some, the ball is tossed up into the air and struck with the bat, almost like baseball.

In all cases, the games were played in an atmosphere of teamwork and vigorous competition. Weapons of war were laid aside and the many descriptions of Native Americans playing these team sports make it clear that the games almost always ended in an atmosphere of friendship and mutual respect. No one seemed to hold a grudge for any injuries received in the playing of these games.

Many of those ideas about team sports are now a part of the modern world. Our children play together and learn to cooperate so that their side can succeed in a game of basketball, football, soccer, or field hockey. But there are still some important differences between the American Indian view of sports and the way sports are seen today. For one, sports have now become big business. A few people become extremely wealthy and famous through their ability to play a sport such as basketball or football. Sometimes only the most talented players are allowed to play, even in sports designed for young people, such as Little League baseball or Pop Warner football. We forget the old Native American rule that everyone can play.

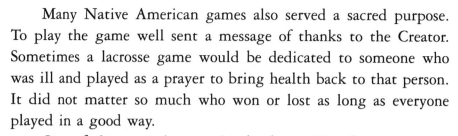

Many Native American games also served a sacred purpose. To play the game well sent a message of thanks to the Creator. Sometimes a lacrosse game would be dedicated to someone who was ill and played as a prayer to bring health back to that person. It did not matter so much who won or lost as long as everyone played in a good way.

One of the many lessons this book provides for young people—in addition to sharing some stories and games that we think they will enjoy—is an introduction to two ideas that are at the heart of American Indian traditions of playing games. The first is that we need to be inclusive. Everyone can play at their own ability. These games are not just meant for the talented few. They are for everyone.

The second is that winning is not the most important thing in a game. The joy of playing, the lessons that we learn from playing together with a good heart, the strength of mind and body and spirit that we gain from playing—those things are always more important than winning.

The Ball Game Between the Animals and the Birds

(MOHAWK)

Long ago, the birds and the animals decided to play a game of lacrosse. All those who could fly would be on one team. All those who could crawl or run would be on the other team.

When they came to the ballfield, they divided up into their two sides. Eagle, Hawk, and Owl were the captains of the birds' team. They called out all of those who would be on their team. Bear, Turtle, and Wolf were the leaders of the animals. They, too, called out those who would be on their side.

When the sides were chosen, two little creatures remained in the middle of the field. They were so small that the animals had not chosen them.

"May we play on your team?" they asked the animals.

"You are too small to be of any use," Wolf replied. Bear and Turtle agreed.

So the two small creatures went to the side of the birds. "The animals will not have us," they said. "Let us play upon your team."

"But you have no wings," said Hawk. "How can you be on our team without wings?"

"Perhaps you can give us wings?" asked the two small creatures.

"We can try to do that," Eagle said.

"That is true," said Owl.

So, Hawk, Owl, and Eagle took the skin from an old drum. They cut it apart and fastened it between the front legs and the back legs on each side of the first small creature. That little creature jumped up into the air, flapped his wings, and flew. That is how Bat got his wings.

"Flying Squirrel caught the ball in his lacrosse stick. He threw it to Bat."

There was not enough leather left to make wings for the second little creature.

"Maybe you can stretch my skin to make wings?" the little creature asked.

"We will try," said Eagle.

Then Hawk and Owl grabbed the loose skin on each side of the little creature. They pulled and pulled on it. They stretched it out. That little creature ran up to the top of a tall tree, jumped off, spread his legs out, and glided on the wind to land on the trunk of another tree far away. He was now Flying Squirrel.

"Now that you have wings," Eagle said to them, "you can be on our side. But you are still small and might be hurt. Wait in this tree until later on in the game. Then maybe you can come in and play."

Now the big ball game began. Bat and Flying Squirrel sat in the tree and watched, holding their little lacrosse sticks.

It was a hard fought game. The two sides were evenly matched. First one would score a goal and then the other. The score was tied and it seemed as if neither side would win. As soon as the sun set, the game would be over.

Just then, as the sun was about to set, the animals got the ball. Deer, the fastest runner of all, raced straight toward the goal of the birds. Just as Deer threw the ball toward the net, a little shape came gliding down. It was Flying Squirrel.

Flying Squirrel caught the ball in his lacrosse stick. He threw it to Bat. Bat caught the ball and began to fly toward the animals' goal. He ducked and dodged so no one could catch him. Just as the sun went down, he scored the final goal.

So it was the two smallest ones, Bat and Flying Squirrel, who won the game for the birds. Ever since then, on summer nights, just when the sun starts to set, Bat and Flying Squirrel come out again to see if they can help win another game.

"Those two birds flew the father and son back to the earth."

The Ball Players in the Sky

(PASSAMAQUODDY)

Long ago there was an old sachem named Edge of the Sky. His wife had died, leaving him alone with their son, Morning Star. Although Edge of the Sky loved the boy very much, he seldom had time to spend with him and they were never able to play games together. So Morning Star often left his father's wigwam, not returning until the end of the day.

One evening, Morning Star remained away from his father's wigwam so late that the old man became worried. The stars were already out in the sky. He went to look for his son and found him walking back across the wide field at the edge of the village.

"Where have you been, son?" Edge of the Sky asked.

"I was playing ball," Morning Star said. "My friends wanted me to keep playing all night, but I told them I had to return home."

Edge of the Sky was puzzled. He had seen none of the other boys in the village and he wondered who it was that his son was playing with. He decided that he would follow his son the next day to see who his playmates were.

When the next day came, however, Edge of the Sky found himself too busy to keep watch on his son. As the sachem of the village, Edge of the Sky had to help other people with their problems. Once again, the end of the day came and his son returned to their lodge, even later than before.

"My friends and I were playing ball again," the boy said. "They wanted me to come with them and play on their ballfield, but I told them I had to return home."

Now Edge of the Sky was a little worried. Perhaps these were boys from another village. But when he asked if any boys from the nearby villages had visited his people everyone told him no. Again, he decided that he would follow his son the next day.

But that day and the day that followed were the same. People came to Edge of the Sky with their problems. Two brothers wanted to use the dugout canoe they had made together. One wanted to take it on the river, but the other wanted to take it on the lake. A mother and daughter had an argument—each one claiming that the other was not bringing in her share of firewood. Such problems were common in a village and it was the sachem's job to listen and give advice so that the problems could be resolved. But because he was so busy helping others with their problems, Edge of the Sky continued to neglect his own son. He did not follow him to see who these strange ball players were.

On the fourth night, Morning Star did not return home at all. Edge of the Sky was truly worried now. He took a torch of dried bark and went to the ballfield to look for his boy. There was no sign of his son at the ballfield, but there was something very strange there. Edge of the Sky had never seen anything like it before. There was a trail of glowing footprints on the ground. They shone like stars.

Edge of the Sky began to follow that trail. He was certain his son had gone that way with his new friends. The trail led north toward the mountains and then rose right up into the sky. Edge of the Sky stayed on the trail and found himself in the skyland.

In front of him was a great wigwam. In front of it stood a tall sachem. Upon the tall sachem's head was a bright light.

"I have come to find my son," Edge of the Sky said.

"Ah," said the sky sachem, "your son was lonely. You were too busy to be with him. So our boys played ball with him. They asked him to come and play upon our field. He is there now, playing happily. Perhaps he will stay here forever."

The sky sachem looked toward the field where the sky people played ball. Edge of the Sky looked there, too. He could not see people there. All that he saw were numerous lights, dancing up and down as they played their game with a ball that was made of fire.

"Do you know which of those ball players is your son?" asked the sky sachem. "If you do, then he can return home with you. If not, he will remain here in the sky."

Edge of the Sky looked hard at the dancing lights. Then he smiled. He knew which one was his boy.

"My son is the brightest of all those lights," Edge of the Sky said.

The tall sky sachem smiled. "It is so," he said. "Call your son to you."

"Morning Star," Edge of the Sky called.

The brightest of the lights broke away from the others and came toward him. When that light was close, it became his son.

"Father," said Morning Star, "I am glad that you came to get me."

Then two great birds flew down. Morning Star climbed onto one and Edge of the Sky onto the other. Those two birds flew the father and son back to the earth. There they lived happily together. And even though he continued to help his people when they needed him, Edge of the Sky never again neglected his son. From that day on, they often played games together.

To this day, the people play the game that the sky people taught Morning Star. Some nights you can still see the children playing their game in the northern sky. Some call them the Northern Lights, but we know them as Wababanal, the Ball Players Made of Light.

Southern tribes usually used two small, light racquets, while northern tribes usually used one long, heavy racquet.

Choctaw woven leather ball.

Pima stone ball, usually covered with mesquite gum/pitch.

Anishinabe doubleballs were sometimes made of straight sticks or bones with a cord of plant fiber or hide used to tie the sticks together.

Ball Games

The balls used in Native games were made of a variety of materials, including wood, stone, bone, and even inflated animal bladders. In most cases, though, balls were constructed of leather strips or strings wrapped tightly around a central core.

Baseballs were once made in that same manner. Among such Native peoples of Mexico and Central America as the Aztecs, Toltecs, and Mayas, balls were made from the bouncy dried sap of the rubber tree. Modern sports such as soccer and basketball, in which a rubber ball is used, owe a lot to the Central American invention of the rubber ball. In fact, a game that combined elements of basketball and soccer was popular in many parts of Central America. Sometimes played on a court made of earth or stone and sunk below ground level, the objective of the game was to knock the rubber ball through an elevated stone hoop.

Many kinds of ball games were invented by the Native peoples of North America. Most of those ball games fit into one of the following four categories:

1. **Racquetball**—games in which the ball is tossed and caught by a racket. The objective is to score a goal by throwing or carrying the ball between the goal posts, which may consist of two upright poles, two poles leaned against each other to form an inverted V, or two upright poles with a cross horizontal pole fastened between them. Lacrosse is the best-known descendant of this widely popular game.

2. **Doubleball**—games in which two balls (or sometimes two sticks) are fastened together to be tossed and caught by a stick.

In the northern parts of the continent, the balls used for the game were made of such things as carved pieces of wood, leather, or other material wrapped and tied to make a ball.

3. **Shinny**—games in which the ball is struck with a stick, often curved at the end, to knock the ball through the air or roll it along the ground. As with the racquetball games, the objective is to strike the ball through the goal posts. Field hockey and ice hockey are said to owe at least part of their origin to shinny.

Arapaho shinny balls.

Playing fields for both shinny and stickball could be as long as three hundred feet, with teams having as many as one hundred players each.

Ball races helped young people develop strong bodies and develop acute mental awareness. Only the nations of the Southwest and parts of California and northern Mexico seem to have played this game.

4. Ball Races—races requiring each of the runners to kick a ball (or a stick, or a pair of sticks tied together) ahead of them as they run on a fixed course. Pairs or large groups of runners, each with their ball individually marked, would take part in these races. Unlike the first three types of ball games, the objective is not to score goals, but to be the first to cross a finish line. Also unlike the first three types of games, which were played in various forms throughout much of North America, ball races were largely found in the southwest.

Following are a number of ball games that are fun to play. Each of these games is based on the way it was played in various Native American nations.

Doubleball

In many places doubleball was a game played by the women and girls, while lacrosse was played by the men and boys. Both lacrosse and doubleball require teamwork, strategy, good hand and eye coordination, balance, and the endurance to run back and forth on a large playing field. Both games emphasize the inclusion of everyone in the game—not just the strongest or most skillful players.

Like lacrosse, doubleball is set up with a goal at either end of the field of play. The field may be of almost any size. Teams may

Except for the Pacific and Northwest coastal areas, doubleball was usually played by women. Girl teams were highly valued in Native culture.

also be of any size, but should be equal. In the old days, lacrosse and doubleball games were sometimes played with one goal in one village and the other goal in the next village. Generally, you will want to set up a field at least fifty feet wide and one hundred feet long. Each player in the game is equipped with a stick about an arm's length with a slight curve on one end. Each player uses either one or two sticks. Our version uses a single stick per player.

When playing the game, teammates must work together to carry and pass the doubleball, two balls contained in leather, toward their opponents' goal. In order to score, a player must hit or throw the doubleball against the opposing goal, a large pole. In a variant form using a horizontal goal, the doubleball must land balanced on the goal stick. Doubleball is a fast-paced game. Teams must be able to advance quickly toward the other goal while being just as quick to defend their own goal when the ball changes hands.

A doubleball made out of sticks and an example of a bladderball.

Suggested Rules

Although doubleball, like lacrosse, originally had virtually no rules, it is a good idea to implement a few basic rules and safety measures. Because this is a game that uses sticks, no stick-to-body contact should be allowed.

1. Stick-to-stick contact must be limited, especially deliberately hitting another's stick to knock the ball free. Again, striking an opponent with the stick is not allowed. To enforce this rule, it is suggested that a player be given a foul the first time he or she hits an opponent with the stick. If it happens a second time, the striker must leave the game for a set period of time.

2. Body contact should also be limited, although it is often hard to avoid, especially when contesting for balls on the ground.

3. Intentionally tripping or knocking other players to the ground should be strongly discouraged.

4. Once a player clearly has the ball, the others must give that player some space to either try to run with it or pass it. Or, once a player has the ball, he or she can move freely until touched by another player (not with a stick). Then he or she is given the opportunity and space to attempt to pass the doubleball to a teammate.

Equipment

Although the simplest "doubleballs" were two sticks tied together by a cord, we suggest that two tennis balls be used for this game.

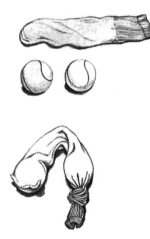

The simplest way to quickly make them into a doubleball is to insert the tennis balls into a sock and tie one end. A more sophisticated doubleball can be made (again with tennis balls for the stuffing) by sewing together a figure 8–shaped piece of leather with the two balls inside pouches at either end and a doubled narrow strip about six inches long at the center.

It is strongly suggested that players wear some sort of eye protection. Padded gloves and safety helmets (such as those worn in lacrosse, or bicycle helmets) can add extra safety.

Two easy steps to making a doubleball.

Blanketball

This game, which combines elements of the ball race and doubleball, is for teams. Each team has a doubleball that is individually colored or marked.

Spread out a blanket at either end of the field or the gymnasium in which the game is to be played. One blanket is the goal for Team A and the other is the goal for Team B. The objective is

Blanketball represents a type of game that taught children about rules, sharing, taking turns, and physically working hard to assist others.

to kick your doubleball onto the blanket that is your goal while trying to prevent the other team from scoring the same way by kicking their doubleball onto their own goal.

Suggested Rules

As with doubleball, any rules should take into account the safety of the children while permitting them as much freedom as possible in playing the game. Because both teams are trying to score at the same time, each with their own doubleball, players have to be on offense and defense at the same time—this can be a game of strategy. For very small children, hard blocking should be discouraged. It is also a good idea to prohibit the intentional tripping of other players.

1. Only your feet or legs can be used to move the ball by kicking or tossing it. No hands allowed in either advancing your ball or blocking the other team's ball!

2. Players are not allowed to step on the blankets that serve as goals.

3. A goal is scored when the doubleball comes to rest on the blanket. Striking the blanket or bouncing off it is not enough.

4. Players are allowed to kick or toss their own ball or their opponents' ball with their feet, but they can only score a point with their own doubleball on their own goal. Be careful, though. If you accidentally knock your opponents' ball onto their goal, you have scored a point for them.

Equipment

If you do not have two doubleballs, you may substitute two tin cans or two sets of sticks tied together. However, a single ball will not work for this game as it will bounce or roll off the blanket too easily.

Batball

This is based on the batted ball game played by a number of different California tribes in the area of Madera County and Yosemite.

Pima wood batball, usually covered with mesquite gum/pitch.

To the Wasama it was called *mula,* a name drawn from the word "mu-lau," the mountain mahogany tree from which the balls and bats were made.

Both teams need to have three or more players. The first two players stand side by side—about twenty feet apart—at the starting line. The other players, each with their own bat, are positioned in relays at set distances in two straight lines between the starting line and the goal. (Among the Wasama, the distance from one player to the next was about five hundred feet.) The two starting players toss their balls up and hit them, trying to

The team sport of *mula* or batball is an exciting combination of skills used in golf, baseball, field hockey, and foot racing.

reach the next player on their team. If the ball doesn't reach the next player, then Player #1 must advance and strike the ball on the ground toward Player #2 on their team. When it reaches Player #2, he or she can pick up the ball and hit it toward Player #3 on their team. The last player in line must hit the ball over the goal. The team with the fewest total strokes to cross the goal wins. Each player must stay within their own territory when advancing the ball.

Equipment

If you wish, you could play this game with bats made of curved sticks cut from tree limbs and two balls made of round pieces of wood wrapped in leather. However, batball can easily be played with two softballs and standard ball bats. For younger children, plastic balls and plastic bats could be used. It is best to use a ball that does not travel too far when hit.

Stickball

Based on the Wabanaki form of shinny, this game can be played with curved sticks made from tree limbs and a fist-sized ball made of tightly wrapped cloth sewed into a piece of deerskin, or with standard hockey sticks and a softball. The game can be played on any level playing field including a sandy beach.

Cheyenne leather stickball.

The game begins by placing the ball into a hole about six inches deep and one foot in diameter in the middle of the field. If played on a beach, the ball can be buried in the sand so that it is out of sight. The two goals, which can be placed either side by side or at opposite ends of the field, are holes dug into the ground. The holes should be about six inches deep and two feet in diameter.

The two opposing teams stand twenty feet apart. At the signal, both teams go for the ball, attempting to dig it out of the hole with their sticks. Each side attempts to score a goal while preventing their opponents from scoring. Whenever a ball falls into a team's goal and remains there, that team scores a point—no matter who hit it there. Whenever a goal is scored, the ball is taken back to the center of the field and placed back into the hole.

A modified version of this game can be played indoors by younger children using sticks made of cardboard, a cloth ball, and three plastic rings or Hula-Hoops placed on the floor as the two goals and the center hole.

Suggested Rules

1. Both teams should be of equal size.

2. The ball can only be touched by the stick.

3. The first side to score an agreed-upon number of goals wins.

4. The ball must land in the goal and remain there to score a point. Opponents can try to block the ball before it

The Wabanaki game of stickball begins with the ball in a hole in the middle of the field, halfway between the opposing goals.

reaches the goal, but cannot stand in the goal or reach into it to hook the ball out.

5. Stick-to-body contact and tripping are not allowed.

Ball Races

Set up a circular course outdoors or in a gymnasium. Using a double-ball or two sticks tied together, two or more players race against each other. (Mark the doubleballs or sticks so that they can be told apart.)

Suggested Rules

1. No hands are allowed—the ball must be kicked using only feet.
2. All players must begin with their ball resting on the ground in front of them.
3. Follow the set course, kicking your ball ahead of you as you run.
4. Only kick your own ball and do not purposefully interfere with an opponent's ball.
5. The first to kick the ball across the finish line wins.

The Zuni kick-stick race was a team race run over a tough twenty-five-mile course, with such natural hazards as sand, rocks, brush, and hills.

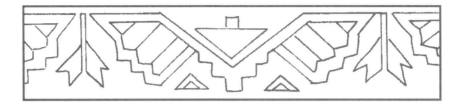

Bowl Games
and Other
Games of Chance

Everyone Needs Luck: Games of Chance in Native Cultures

Today, thanks to Indian casinos, Native American communities are often associated with the controversy of gambling. But Native American games of chance were popular long before bingo and gambling casinos. In many cases, the original Native American "gambling" games were associated with traditional ceremonies. The objective in such games was not for one person to get rich. Instead, bowl games might be played to celebrate the victory of life over death and the end of winter. Having fun was more important than just winning material goods. The community aspect of Native games of chance is very evident when you watch two sides taking part in such games, as many Native American nations still do to this day. Each side has their own chants and songs to encourage their players and bring them luck.

One form of the bowl game that was played in Massachusetts was called "hubbub" by the European settlers who observed it being played. The Native people gathered around and would repeatedly chant the word "Hub" until the one holding the bowl with its five bone dice was ready to take his turn. Some say that the modern word "hubbub," meaning "a confusion of sounds," is of Celtic origin—a game of hubbub was certainly a loud and noisy occasion! William Wood described it like this in 1634: "Hubbub is five small bones in a small smooth tray, the bones be like a die, but something flatter, black on one side and white on the other, which they place on the ground against which violently thumping the platter, the bones mount changing color with the windy whisking of their hands to and fro; which action in that sport they much use, smiting themselves on the breast, and thighs, crying out, Hub, Hub, Hub; they may be heard play at this game a quarter of a mile off" (*New England's Prospect,* London, University of Massachusets Press, 1977).

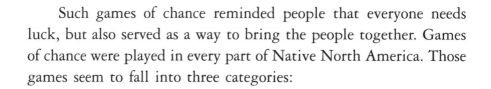

Such games of chance reminded people that everyone needs luck, but also served as a way to bring the people together. Games of chance were played in every part of Native North America. Those games seem to fall into three categories:

1. Bowl games—dice made of seeds, bone, wood, or stones are thrown or shaken inside a bowl or on a tray held by the player.

2. Stick dice games—marked sticks are tossed onto the ground or another stationary surface.

3. Guessing games—two players (each representing a side) sit facing each other. One player hides one or more small objects such as buttons, seeds, and pieces of wood or bone. Then the other player must guess where the object or objects are hidden.

The activities in this section are based on traditional games of chance that were played on the American continent, although the rules have been slightly changed or simplified to make them easier to understand.

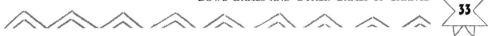

The Good Mind's Game

(ONONDAGA)

Long ago, it is said, the Good Mind had to play a game of high stakes. If the Good Mind lost, life on Earth would end. Some say it was his Grandmother who decided this fate. Her daughter had died giving birth to the Good Mind and his brother Flint. So her heart was sad and she wanted all life to end.

The game to be played was *Tayuneoowahes,* Throwing the Bowl, the plumstone game. It was a simple game. Six plumstones were placed in a big wooden bowl. Those stones were flattened and painted white on one side and black on the other. Each player would strike the bowl against the ground so that the stones flew up. If the stones landed with either all the white sides up or all the black sides up, that would gain *Ohentak,* a field, or one point.

The Good Mind was worried. He was always a friend of life and had tried to make this world a good place, even though his brother Flint had tried to make life difficult. How could the Good Mind win this game and make sure that life would continue?

That is when the Chickadees, those little birds whose heads are white and black, spoke to him.

"Use our heads," they said. "We will help you win."

So the Good Mind did as they said. He took the heads of the Chickadees and placed them in the bowl. Then he handed the bowl to his Grandmother.

"You may go first," he said.

His Grandmother struck the bowl against the ground. The six black and white plumstones that were actually the heads of the Chickadees flew up into the air and landed with three white sides and three black sides showing. Each time she tried, it ended that way. She made no points at all.

"The black and white stones that were actually the heads of the Chickadees flew up into the air. They sang as they flew."

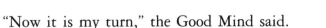

"Now it is my turn," the Good Mind said.

He struck the bowl against the ground. The black and white stones that were actually the heads of the Chickadees flew up into the air. They sang as they flew and when they landed they were all black side up. They had gained *Ohentak* and made one point for the Good Mind. So it was each time he struck the bowl. The Chickadees' heads flew up singing and landed scoring a point. The Good Mind won the game and life continued on.

So it is that to this day the bowl game is played, although nowadays peachstones are used. Life continues on this Earth and the Chickadees sing their victory song. Playing the bowl game reminds the people that all life is a sacred gift. It reminds them of how, long ago, those small birds helped the Good Mind preserve all life.

"While the two sides played, Coyote stood in the middle between them."

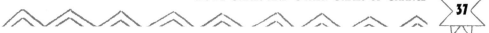

Kesitce:
The Moccasin Game

(DINEH [NAVAJO])

In the old times it was not yet certain whether day would be longer than night or night longer than day. So the animals and birds had a meeting to make a decision about this great concern. That council met at twilight.

The animals and birds of the day spoke. They said that the sun should shine all the time. The animals and birds of the night spoke. They said that the sun should never rise again. Neither side could agree with the other.

"Let us play a game of *kesitce* to decide," someone said.

Everyone agreed it was a good idea. A fire was lit and the teams sat on opposite sides. They flipped a piece of wood that was dark on one side and light on the other to see which team would go first. It fell with the dark side up and so the animals of the night were the first to hide the stone.

The moccasins were placed side by side in the sand. The night creatures lifted up the blanket so that the day creatures could not see where they hid the stone and they sang the same song that the Dine people sing to this day when they play *kesitce.* Owl was the one who was hiding the stone, for he was one of the best at the game.

While the two sides played, Coyote stood in the middle between them. As long as the night creatures were winning, Coyote said he was on their side.

"Ah-ha," Coyote said, "we who are creatures of the night are doing well."

The night creatures won again and again. Then Wind, who wanted to help the day creatures, came and whispered in the ear of Magpie.

"Owl is cheating. He is keeping the stone in his claws."

So, when it was Magpie's turn to take the stick and tap the moccasin where the stone was hidden, Magpie struck Owl's claws instead. Owl dropped the stone. Now it was the turn of the day creatures to hide the stone and they began to win.

"This is good," Coyote said. "We who are the creatures of the day are now winning!"

Coyote, though, did not fool anyone. That is why, to this day, neither the creatures of the day nor the creatures of the night trust Coyote.

The game went back and forth between the two sides. Neither one seemed able to win it all. The two sides were even in the number of counters each had won. Then Wind came and whispered again to Magpie.

"Sing the Dawn Song," Wind whispered.

"Qua-yei-ka, Qua-yei-ka!" Magpie sang. "Dawn is here, Dawn is here!"

As soon as he sang those words, the light of dawn appeared. With the light of the new day, the game had to end. All the animals and birds quickly went back to their homes. So it is, to this day, that day and night are of equal lengths, for the two sides never again came together to finish their game.

How Day and Night Came to Be

(JICARILLA TINNEH [APACHE])

In the world before this one, it was dark. The people used torches to see their way around, but they longed for more light. The animals and birds of the day also wanted more light. However, the night animals and birds thought that even the light from the torches was too bright. They wanted it always to remain dark.

The two sides argued about this for a long time. Finally, they decided that they would play *kayonti,* the stone-guessing game, to decide.

The creatures of the night hid the stone well, but Magpie, who was playing on the side of the people and other day creatures, had very sharp eyes. He could see which hollow stick had the stone and he told the people which stick to choose. So the people won the first game. As soon as they won, the Morning Star came out in the sky. Black Bear, who was on the side of the night creatures, ran off to hide in a dark place.

Again, the night creatures hid the stone in one of the hollow sticks. This time Quail was the one who helped the people. He saw where the stone was and told them which stick to choose. This time when they won the first light before dawn showed itself in the sky. Now Brown Bear, who was on the side of the night creatures, ran off to hide.

A third time the night creatures hid the stick. Once again, Magpie and Quail helped the people to choose right. Now the eastern sky began to grow bright and Mountain Lion ran off to hide.

A fourth time the stone was hidden and, just as before, Magpie and Quail used their sharp eyes. "It is there!" they said and the people chose right once more. The sun came up and Owl flew away to hide.

"The sun came up and Owl flew away to hide."

That is where the game ended. The day creatures and the night creatures never came back again together to finish that game. Because it was only half over, the sun goes down every day and night comes back. But every morning, the sun rises once more and it remains in the sky. So half the time it is day and half the time it is night. It has been that way ever since.

Games of Chance

Hubbub

Hubbub is a game that directly involves two players, but may involve a large number of others divided into two sides to "back up" the principal players. A similar game played among the Micmac people is called *woltes*. Each side can choose either to have one primary person "strike the bowl" or to take turns among teammates.

In the bowl game of the Sauk and Fox (hubbub), the dice were shaped like turtles. The best throw was to make the "turtles" land upright.

In a "guessing game" each side gets two of four fat bones—one with a stripe and one without. Then a player hides the bones in their hands, folds their arms and puts their hands way under their armpits, and rocks back and forth to the beat of a drum. When the drum ends, they bring their fists out, with the backs of the hands facing up. A member of the other team guesses which hand has either the striped or unstriped bone in it (one team guesses striped, the other unstriped), and then the player shows where the bone actually is. Two pointed sticks are stuck in the ground, one for each team. When a guess is correct, the winning team gets a point and a small stick (either striped or unstriped) is placed in a line next to the team's ground marker. Whichever team gains all five of their sticks lined-up next to their ground marker first is the winner.

To play hubbub you need a blanket; a wooden bowl; five round, flat dice marked with a black pattern on one side and unmarked on the other; fifty-two sticks of the same size, all about nine inches long; and one slightly larger stick which is shaped like an arrow. The sticks are used as counters, with the fifty-two sticks representing the "people" in the village and the stick shaped like an arrow representing the "sagamon," the village leader. A bowl-shaped basket might be substituted for the bowl. The dice could be made from bone, stones, dried peach pits, wood (pogs, for example), or even bottle caps.

To decide who goes first, one of the dice can be tossed up. If it lands black side up, one side goes first. If it lands unmarked side up, the other side goes first.

Small children can play stick toss with as few as five sticks. One should be marked as the "win stick." The sticks are gently thrown like pick-up sticks. When the marked stick lands on top, the person that threw the "win stick" wins.

The sticks are placed to one side where an impartial judge, the "Lodgekeeper," keeps score. When one side scores, the Lodgekeeper gives them a certain number of sticks. If the "lodge" is empty (no sticks are left), then the Lodgekeeper takes sticks back from the opposite side's winnings. The Lodgekeeper also acts as a referee. If there is a question about whether or not all the dice flew up, for example, the Lodgekeeper decides.

The last stick to be won out of those held by the Lodgekeeper is the sagamon, the last one in the village to come out of the lodge. However, the sagamon can only be won on a double score (see page 45). When one side has won all of the sticks and the sagamon, the game is over. If a certain amount of time is allotted to the game, then the side with the most sticks wins.

A blanket is placed on the ground between the two players, who sit on their knees or cross-legged across from each other. The first player takes the bowl and begins to shake it, moving it about until ready to strike the bowl with both hands against the blanket—making the dice fly up into the air. While the player is getting ready to do this, all of those on that player's side can chant together, "Hub, Hub, Hub, Hub, Hub!" The chant should end in a great shout when the player strikes the bowl onto the blanket.

If the player makes a winning score (5 or 3 + 2), that same player can go again and keep on going until making no score (4 + 1 or one or more of the dice fail to stay in the bowl).

Suggested Rules

1. The bowl must be held with both hands, fingers and thumbs on the outside.
2. All of the dice must fly up into the air when the bowl is struck down onto the blanket.
3. All of the dice must land back in the bowl or the player does not score and must pass the bowl to the other side.
4. The Lodgekeeper is the scorer and decides whether or not any throw is a fair one.

Scoring

4 of one color, 1 of the other = no score (no sticks)
3 of one color, 2 of the other = single score (two sticks)
5 of one color = double score (four sticks or the sagamon)
No score = whenever one or more of the dice fall outside the bowl

Equipment

1. Blanket.
2. Round wooden bowl or shallow round basket about twelve inches in diameter.
3. Five round dice, all of the same size. They should be about the size of a bottle cap and marked with a dark pattern on one side only.

4. Fifty-three counters, fifty-two of which are nine-inch sticks of the same size, and one of which is the "sagamon" stick, cut slightly larger and shaped like an arrow. The sticks can be made of wood or cardboard.

Moccasin

Moccasin is a popular game of both skill and luck. There are a number of different ways in which the moccasin game can be played. In all of them, the two opposing teams each choose a player who will represent their side each time the stone is hidden. The player hiding the stone is on one side, the player guessing where the stone is hidden is on the other. You can use actual shoes or moccasins to hide the stone or you can make "moccasins" out of cardboard or stiff paper. As with hubbub, you can use sticks as counters.

Each side is given forty counter sticks at the start. The game continues until one side has won all the sticks. Among the different tribal nations of the southwest, the moccasin game is played at night near the fire. That is when old stories say that the first game took place between the creatures of day and the creatures of night. It is also harder to guess where a stone is hidden at night when it is more difficult to see.

Suggested Rules

1. The two sides sit in two groups four feet apart on either side of an imaginary fire. (If played outside at night, a real fire can be between the two sides. Indoors, a symbolic fire in the form of a circle of stones or a picture of a fire can be placed on the floor between them.) One side is the Day Side. One side is the Night Side. They are not allowed to "cross to the other side of the fire."

2. Each side chooses one player to represent them as the "Guesser" or the "Hider." One player keeps on guessing or hiding until they lose.

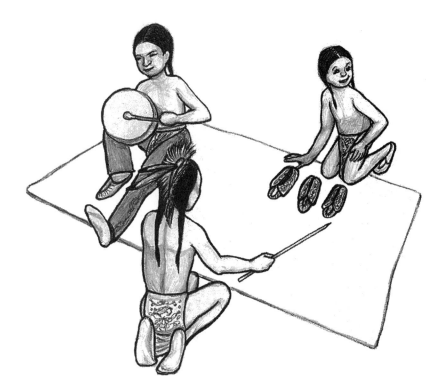

Two Anishinabe boys have hidden a ball in one of the moccasins on the blanket. One of them plays a drum and sings to distract their opponent, who is trying to guess where the ball is.

3. The player who is the Hider takes the stone, shows it to the other team, and then begins to hide the stone. The Hider can move the stone from one hand to the other, and then pretend to place it in one moccasin or another. The stone can be hidden in one of the three moccasins or kept in one of the Hider's hands. In the old-style games, there was not a time limit to this game. However, contemporary versions keep the game moving by giving the Hider only about twenty seconds.

4. While the hiding team is deciding where to hide the stone, everyone on the guessing team slowly counts out aloud together from 1 to 20.

5. When the final count is reached, the Hider must place his or her hands down on the ground behind the moccasins.

6. The Guesser must then indicate his or her choice by reaching forward and tapping it lightly with the guessing stick. However, it is important to note that the Guesser *never* wants to find the stone in a moccasin on the first try.

7. The hiding side continues to hide the stone until the other side makes a winning guess.

Scoring

If the Guesser chooses the right moccasin on the first try, no points are scored. The Guesser is not allowed to guess again. The hiding side gets 4 points and is allowed to hide the stone once more.

If the Guesser chooses the right moccasin on the second try, the guessing side scores 4 points. The hiding side now becomes the guessing side.

If the Guesser chooses the right moccasin on the third try, the guessing side scores 10 points. The hiding side now becomes the guessing side.

If, at any time, the Guesser taps one of the Hider's hands and finds the stone, this is a winning choice. The guessing side scores 6 points and the hiding side becomes the guessing side.

If the Guesser cannot find the stone after the maximum of three tries, the hiding side wins 6 points and gets to hide the stone again.

Equipment

1. Eighty counter sticks, forty for each side.

2. One "stone," which can actually be a stone, a large button, a stick, or some other round object about the size of a quarter that can be hidden in a player's hand. (In stick games, where a stick is concealed in the player's hand, the sticks are usually about three inches long.)

3. Three moccasins or three identical shoes either real or made of cardboard or thick paper that is rolled into a cone and then stapled to make a "moccasin."

4. One guessing stick that will be used to indicate the moccasin or hand chosen by tapping it with the stick. The guessing stick could be a long thin round of wood (these can be purchased cheaply at any hardware or hobby store) or a yardstick. The guessing stick must be at least three feet long.

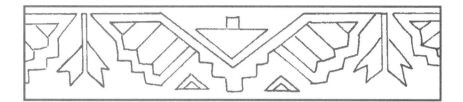

Games
of
Skill

The Eye of the Hawk:
Games of Skill Among Native People

Games of skill often focus on those activities that require the same hand-eye coordination that would be needed for survival. It is easy to see the connection between throwing a spear-shaped stick accurately or shooting an arrow at a moving hoop and being a good hunter.

But even such seemingly simple games as Hoop and Pole, where one player rolls a small hoop and the other tries to throw a pole that is about nine feet long so that it goes into the hoop and stops it, could be very complicated. For example, the hoop might be divided into four colors, with the color touched by the upper part of the spear determining the score. Or the spear itself might have different markings on it and the score would depend upon which marking the hoop touched. The Tinneh (Apache) game of Hoop and Pole was incredibly complex in its scoring system, which was based on the markings on both the pole and the hoop.

Sometimes the hoop would be netted or webbed and the score would depend on what part of the web was pierced by the pole. Other times, hoops were made very small. While the Navajo and Apache used hoops that ranged from six inches to ten inches in diameter, the Mesquakie of the Great Lakes region used hoops made of elm bark that were as little as two inches in diameter.

All of the activities in this section make use of the hoop. Remember that the hoop is a very important symbol in Native cultures. The hoop stands for the sacred circle of life. As Black Elk, a famous holy man of the Lakota Sioux, once said, "Everything an Indian does is in a circle." Black Elk then went on to point out how many things in nature are round, from the shape of the moon and sun and the nests of birds to the cycle of the seasons. So, when Native children played games with the hoop, they were also being reminded of the sacred nature of life, where in all things are connected in a great circle.

"You can still hear the roll of thunder and see the tongue of lightning flash as they shout and play."

How the Two Brothers Followed the Hoop

(CADDO)

There were two boys who lived alone with their father and mother in a lodge next to a big pecan tree. Once they had lived in a large village with many people. However, people began to disappear. They would go out to hunt or gather food and never come back. Now only these four family members were left.

Then, one day, the mother went out to dig for roots and did not return. The father looked long and hard for his wife, but he could not find her. He was very sad.

"My boys," he said to his two sons, "surely the ones who eat human beings have now caught your mother. Now only the three of us remain. When I go out to hunt, you must always stay close to our lodge."

"We will do so," said the first boy. But the second brother said nothing.

While their father was gone, the boys played games. The second brother took a strip of elm bark and shaped it into a circle that he wrapped with deerskin to make a small hoop. Then he made two arrows. One arrow was black and the other was blue.

"Now we can play," he said to his brother.

And so they played. One brother would roll the hoop and the other would try to strike it with his arrow to stop the hoop. They liked this game very much and they played it every day. They became very good at stopping the little hoop by putting their arrows right into the center. Each day they would do so from farther and farther away.

One day, Second Brother rolled the hoop. First Brother missed it with his arrow and the hoop kept rolling. It rolled and rolled, going faster and faster, leaving a track behind it in the soft earth and the grass. It rolled out of sight over the top of a hill.

First Brother was very sad. "We have lost our hoop," he said.

"Do not worry," Second Brother said, wrapping a buffalo calf robe around his shoulders and tying his pouch to his belt. "We can follow its trail."

The two brothers began to follow the trail the hoop made. They went over one hill and then another and another. Soon they were very far away from their father's lodge.

They traveled until the sun was in the middle of the sky. Second Brother looked around. "We have come halfway," he said. "Now we must do something."

Then Second Brother reached into his pouch and took out a nut from the pecan tree that grew by their lodge. "I will plant this," he said, "and we will pray for help."

Second Brother planted the pecan and the two boys prayed for help. As they did so, a pecan tree grew up. It grew taller and taller, reaching high into the sky.

Second Brother took off his buffalo calf robe. "Now," he said, "I am going to climb to the top of this tree. Sit here under the tree and do not look up. My bones will fall down from the top of the tree, one by one. Take them and place them under my buffalo calf robe. Then shoot your black arrow at the robe and shout for me to get up before the arrow hits me. Do as I say and all will be well."

Second Brother began to climb up into the tree. First Brother sat with his back against the tree and waited. Soon bones began to fall down from the tree. First Brother waited until all of the bones had fallen. Then he covered them with the buffalo calf robe.

"Brother, get up before this arrow hits you!" he shouted. Then he shot the black arrow into the buffalo robe.

Before the arrow struck the robe, Second Brother jumped out from beneath it. He was alive and well and looked much stronger than he had been before.

"Our Sky Father gave me great power," Second Brother said. "Now you must do as I did so that you can gain power, too."

First Brother did just as Second Brother had done. He climbed the tree and his bones fell to the earth one by one. Second Brother covered the bones with the buffalo calf robe and shouted, "Brother, get up before this arrow hits you!"

Then he shot his blue arrow into the buffalo calf robe and First Brother jumped out alive and well. He, too, knew that he had been given great power. He opened his mouth to shout and the sound of thunder came from him and shook the earth.

He was now Thunder Boy.

"Brother," Thunder Boy asked, "what power were you given?"

"I will show you," said Second Brother. "Watch this!" He stuck out his tongue and lightning shot from his mouth.

He was now Lightning Boy.

"What shall we do now?" Thunder Boy asked.

"We must follow the track of our hoop," Lightning Boy answered.

They kept following the track of their hoop through the grass and over the hills. At last they came to the top of a high hill and they saw a wide trail below that looked as if many people had walked upon it. An old man with a kind look on his face was coming toward them along that trail. He held their hoop in his hands.

Thunder Boy began to go down the hill toward the old man. Lightning Boy stopped him.

"That is not an old man," Lightning Boy said. "He is one of those who eats human beings. Use your power, brother."

Thunder Boy opened his mouth and shouted. Thunder rolled around them and the old man dropped the hoop and fell to the ground. When he got up he no longer looked like an old man. He was an Eater of Human Beings with hungry eyes and long, sharp teeth. He turned and began to run away.

"Now use your power, brother," Thunder Boy said.

Lightning Boy opened his mouth and stuck out his tongue. Lightning flashed through the air, struck the Eater of Human Beings, and killed him.

Thunder Boy picked up their hoop. The two brothers continued to walk down the wide trail. Soon they came to a village. Smoke rose above the lodges. The people in the village saw them coming and smiled at them.

"Come and join us!" the people shouted. "It is time to eat!"

Thunder Boy and Lightning Boy looked at each other. Thunder Boy opened his mouth and shouted. Thunder rolled all around and the people in the village fell to the ground. When they stood up, they no longer looked like people. They were all Eaters of Human Beings. Lightning Boy opened his mouth and lightning flashed through the air, killing all of those monsters.

Then the two brothers walked into the village. There were piles of bones everywhere. Those were the bones of all the people who had been eaten. Thunder Boy and Lightning Boy piled the bones together and covered them with the buffalo calf robe. Once again, they shouted.

"Get up before our arrows hit you!"

Then they shot their arrows into the buffalo robe. All the people who had been eaten jumped out alive and well. Among them was the mother of the two boys.

They took their mother back home. Their father was overjoyed to see them and they were all very happy. They lived together for a very long time. Finally, after their parents died of old age, the two brothers left the earth. They took their hoop and arrows and went to live in the sky. They are there to this day, playing their game high above the clouds. You can still hear the roll of thunder and see the tongue of lightning flash as they shout and play.

Hoop Games

Ring and Pin

From the Arctic Ocean to the Gulf of Mexico, one of the most popular games of Native North Americans is the game of Ring and Pin. It is played by little children and grown-ups alike. In its simplest form, a small hoop is attached to a stick with a cord. Holding the stick in one hand, the ring is swung up into the air and the player tries to catch the ring with the stick. When this game is played by two or more people, each player continues to play until he or she does not catch the ring. In this simple form, each catch is worth a point.

However, more than two hundred different varieties of this game have been recorded. Among the Inuit of the far north, the pin may be replaced by an ivory carving in the shape of an animal.

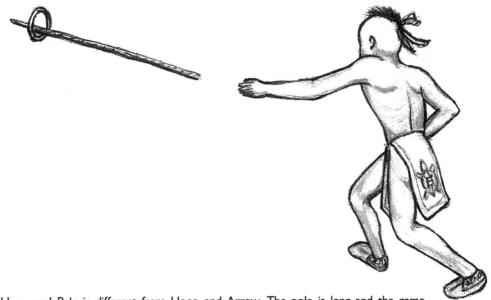

Hoop and Pole is different from Hoop and Arrow. The pole is long and the game can by played to stop the hoop or to have the pole slide through the hoop (as shown).

Two girls enjoy a game of Ring and Pin. This game was known throughout the far Canadian north to the southern parts of Mexico.

The carving is pierced by a number of holes and the player gets a different score depending on which hole the pin enters.

Among the Cree, the string is threaded through a series of bones with a triangle-shaped bone on the end. The bone, which might also be a piece of stiff leather or carved wood, has a number of holes in it of various sizes. As in the Inuit game, the player's score depends on which hole the pin catches. The practice of threading the string through a series of bones or carved pieces of wood is widely practiced around the continent. Among the Pueblo people, dried rings of squash are threaded onto the string. Among the

Abenaki, a bundle of twigs is sometimes substituted for the ring and a long, sharp piece of bone is tied to that bundle to serve as the pin.

Suggested Rules

Here are the rules to play Ring and Pin with two or more people:

1. You may use only one hand.
2. Each player's turn lasts until he or she does not catch the ring with the pin.
3. Each catch counts as 1 point.
4. The first player to reach an agreed-upon number of points (12, for example) wins.

Equipment

A Ring and Pin game may be played with simple materials. A slender stick from six inches to one foot in length can serve as the pin. A ring can be made by bending a coat hanger into a circle, wrapping it back around itself to make a ring that is two inches in diameter. (The same method can be used to make the hoop for the game of Hoop and Pole.) To hold the wire hoop together more securely, wrap electrician's tape or narrow pieces of duct tape around the ring. You can then put on a final layer of colored yarn or leather. Fasten the ring to the stick one-third of the way up from the lower end of the stick with a string that is twelve to eighteen inches long.

To use the ring and pin, hold the pin by its long end in your hand as you would hold a pencil, with the ring hanging down below your fist. Now flip the ring up and attempt to catch it by spearing it with the pin.

More complicated forms of Ring and Pin can be played by changing the ring. The ring can be webbed with string and a higher score given the player when the pin catches the ring in the center. Two or more rings of different sizes can be attached to the string.

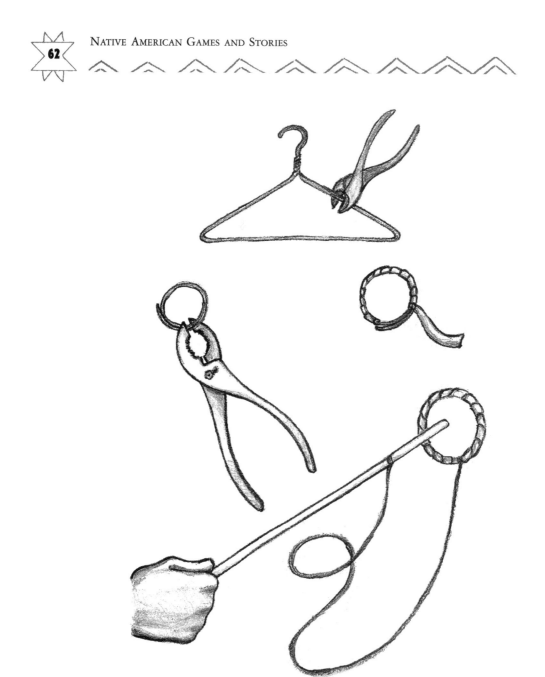

1. A slender stick from six inches to one foot in length can serve as the pin.
2. A ring can be made by bending a coat hanger into a circle, wrapping it back around itself to make a ring that is two inches in diameter. (The same method can be used to make the hoop for the game of Hoop and Pole.) 3. To hold the wire hoop together more securely, wrap electrician's tape or narrow pieces of duct tape around the ring. 4. You can then put on a final layer of colored yarn or leather. 5. Fasten the ring to the stick one-third of the way up from the lower end of the stick with a string that is twelve to eighteen inches long.

Catching the smaller ring wins a score of 2, the larger a score of 1. Among the Inuit of Baffin Island, where the game is called *ajegaung,* a piece of carved ivory or bone takes the place of the ring. The carving, in the shape of a polar bear, has holes in different parts of its body. Each hole gives the player a different score. Among certain other Native nations, such as the Paiute, the dried skull bone of a small animal such as a rabbit would be used.

Hoop and Pole

Hoop and Pole can be played in many different ways. The only equipment needed is a hoop and a number of long slender poles, one for each player. The hoop is rolled by one player while the others throw their poles in an attempt to stop the hoop by hitting it in the center with the pole. Scoring can be as simple as giving a point each time the person throwing the pole pierces the hoop, or a more complicated scoring system can be used. We describe here two different ways to play and score this game. The first is for younger children.

BASIC HOOP AND POLE

Suggested Rules

1. The players with poles are the "throwers." The throwers line up next to each other, about four feet apart, in a straight line. A small circle can be marked on the floor to indicate each thrower's place. The throwers are not allowed to leave their places. They must keep one foot inside the circle at all times.

2. Two players are the "hoop rollers." They stand facing each other. A course can be drawn on the floor showing where they must roll the hoop. The course should be drawn so that it is about six feet away from the line of the throwers. Hoop Roller A rolls the hoop toward Hoop Roller B.

3. As the hoop rolls by the throwers, each tries to throw his or her pole so that it stops the hoop.

4. If a thrower's pole stops the hoop and the hoop falls over and lands touching that pole, the thrower scores 1 point. If no one's pole stops the hoop or if the hoop falls over or goes off the course, no points are scored.

5. Hoop Roller B takes the hoop and rolls it on the course toward Hoop Roller A. They continue alternating until a point is scored.

Hoop and Pole was primarily restricted to men. In some tribes women were forbidden to even watch the game.

6. After a point is scored, the players rotate. Hoop Roller A becomes Hoop Roller B. Hoop Roller B becomes a thrower. The first thrower in line becomes Hoop Roller A.

7. The first player to reach an agreed-upon number of points is the winner.

Equipment

To keep this game safe for younger children, the poles should not be made of wood. The ideal pole for younger children could be made of a pole-shaped three-foot-long piece of foam rubber. If you do not have access to foam rubber, poles can be made from cardboard or heavy construction paper. Cut out pieces that are three feet long and one and one-half inches wide. Tape together two or more pieces to make them stiff enough to throw as a pole. Decorate each pole so that they can be told apart. It may be necessary to weight the end of the pole so that it can be thrown like a spear. This can be done by taping on a piece of foam rubber or cloth. *Do not* make the point of the pole sharp! A plastic Hula-Hoop can be used for this game. A smaller plastic hoop may be substituted to make the game harder.

ADVANCED HOOP AND POLE

Suggested Rules

1. Two players are the "hoop rollers."

2. As in the basic game, the hoop is rolled past a line of "throwers," but the course the hoop is rolled on must be farther away from the line of throwers—twelve feet at a minimum.

3. The throwers attempt to stop the hoop by throwing their poles and piercing the hoop.

4. As with the basic version, players rotate their places after a thrower makes a scoring throw.

Scoring

1. 1 point if the pole remains inside the hoop when the hoop is stopped but no colors match in the hoop and pole.
2. 2 points if the white part of the hoop is resting on top of the white part of the pole.
3. 3 points if the yellow part of the hoop is resting on top of the yellow part of the pole.
4. 4 points if the black part of the hoop is resting on top of the black part of the pole.
5. 5 points if the red part of the hoop is resting on top of the red part of the pole.
6. The first player to reach 20 points wins.

Equipment

The hoop can be made from a coat hanger that is twisted into a circle and then wrapped with tape. The hoop should be from four to six inches in diameter. By using different colors of tape or cloth, the hoop is marked into four equal sections: white, yellow, black, and red.

Alternately, a hoop can be made from bark. Elm, basswood, maple, and ash can all be used for this. However, pulling the bark off a tree will injure the tree or even kill it. Further, only bark that is taken in the spring will be supple enough to make into a hoop. If a tree has been cut or pruned before the leaves come in the spring, you could use its bark. You can tell if the bark is usable if it peels off the tree easily and is moist underneath. Cut a long strip of bark, roll it into the shape of a hoop, and either tie it with cord or sew it together (holes can be made in the rubbery bark with an awl or a sharp-pointed knife). When the bark has dried (usually within twenty-four hours) it will hold that hoop shape. As with the coat hanger, the hoop can then be wrapped or painted to make the four colors.

Nine-foot-long straight saplings are the best material for poles, although long round pieces of wood can be purchased at a lumberyard.

Do not sharpen the ends. Color the end of every pole as follows: the first six inches of the pole white, the next six inches yellow, the next six inches black, the next six inches red. Also mark each pole individually so they can be told apart.

For some tribes the hoop symbolized the sun or the cycles of life. This game was often an integral part of religious rituals and was credited with the power to cure illness.

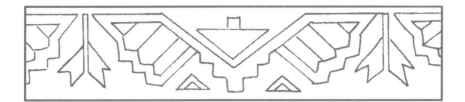

Awareness Games

Hearing the Wind:
Native Awareness

Today, few people make full use of their senses. Our Creator gave us each two ears and two eyes and only one mouth. That should remind us that listening and observing are twice as important as talking. However, we seldom do a really good job of using our ears and eyes. We listen to the radio or to our portable phones and CD players, but we're not very good at listening to each other or to the natural world around us. We look at movies and television and all kinds of technology, but we do not pay close attention to other things around us.

To Native American people, the full use of all the senses, hearing, seeing, smelling, touching, and tasting, was often a matter of life and death. When you live as our Native ancestors used to live, hunting and finding food, finding your way safely through the forest or the desert, recognizing the possibility of danger depended upon using all of one's senses properly. Unfortunately, for modern people, failing to fully use or properly focus our senses can often put us in danger too. If you are not alert when you walk across a street, if you focus more on your portable phone than your driving, if you do not recognize the dangers in walking alone at night in a city park, you can find yourself in just as much trouble today as our ancestors faced in the past.

Because of the importance of full awareness, many of the games that Native children played were designed to strengthen and focus their senses.

"Fly for your lives," that little duck shouted. "Nanabush is killing us!"

Nanabush and the Ducks

(Anishinabe)

Nanabush was out walking around. He had been walking for a long time and he was feeling hungry. Then, as he was walking along, he came to a lake. Way out in the middle of that lake he could see some ducks. They were floating around the ways ducks do, way out there in the lake where no one could get them. But even though those ducks were far away, Nanabush could see that those ducks were fat. They looked like they would be very good to eat.

"Huh," Nanabush said. "It has been a long time since I have done anything for my friends, the ducks. I should honor them with a dance. That is just what I will do. I am going to have a big duck dance at my lodge. Hear me everyone," he said in a loud voice, "I am going to have a big dance for the ducks."

Then Nanabush went back to his lodge to get ready for the dance. He made a nice fire, right in the middle of the floor there inside his wigwam. He got out his big drum and began to play it.

Boom-boom, boom-boom
Boom-boom, boom-boom

You could hear that drum of his from a long ways off. Then Nanabush began to sing. Nanabush's song was almost as loud as the drum. The ducks heard the drum and the song.

"Ah-ha," said the ducks, "Nanabush is having a dance for us at his lodge."

All the ducks came to Nanabush's wigwam. The door flap was propped open and they looked inside. There in the middle of the lodge, just behind the fire, Nanabush sat playing his drum and singing. He smiled when he saw them.

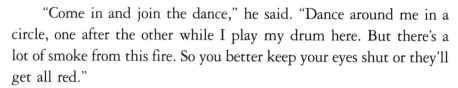

"Come in and join the dance," he said. "Dance around me in a circle, one after the other while I play my drum here. But there's a lot of smoke from this fire. So you better keep your eyes shut or they'll get all red."

The ducks did just as Nanabush told them to do. They closed their eyes as they came in the lodge so their eyes wouldn't get red. They danced around in a circle one after the other while Nanabush played his drum.

Boom-boom, boom-boom
Boom-boom, boom-boom

You know how when you give a party for certain people, sometimes others come who were not invited? It was that way at the party Nanabush gave for the ducks. A great big heron wanted to come to that dance. So he had slipped into Nanabush's lodge. There he was, dancing around and trying to look like a duck. He wasn't doing a very good job of it.

When that heron got close enough, Nanabush reached out with one hand while he kept playing the drum with the other. He grabbed the heron by the neck. He grabbed him so hard that the heron's neck got stretched out and all bent. Herons' necks are all like that to this day. Nanabush pulled that heron in close so he could whisper to him.

"If you want to keep breathing," Nanabush whispered, "you start playing this drum."

The heron took the drumstick and began to play.

Boom-boom, boom-boom
Boom-boom, boom-boom

Nanabush kept on singing, but now he had both hands free. Every now and then as he sang he would yell. And each time he

yelled, he reached out and grabbed a duck and wrung its neck.

Nanabush's plan was working. He might have gotten all of those ducks if it hadn't been for the smallest duck of all. That duck had her eyes closed just like all the others, but she was a good listener. She thought she heard something strange. It was a sound like a muffled squawk! She opened her eyes just a crack. And you know what she saw. She saw Nanabush wringing the neck of the duck he'd just grabbed.

"Fly for your lives!" that little duck shouted. "Nanabush is killing us!"

All those ducks flew for the door of the lodge. The little duck that warned the others was the coot. And you know, even though Nanabush was trying to trick those ducks, he had told them the truth. Because she opened her eyes inside the lodge, the coot's eyes got red from the smoke. All coots still have red eyes to this day. But still, because that little coot was so good at listening, except for the few Nanabush had already caught, all of those ducks got away. That is the story of Nanabush and the ducks.

The following games and activities employ varied awareness skills, often bringing in basic body movements requiring balance and focus. These and similar activities were part of child-rearing among many different Native nations. The skills involved, as we have seen in countless workshops, can aid anyone who wishes to maximize their senses, balance, and awareness—not only in a wilderness setting, but in everyday life.

When stalking, the closer you get to your objective, the slower you go—until it looks like you are hardly moving at all.

Awareness Games

Stalking

Originally used as a hunting skill, this type of walking was used to get close to wild animals. It also increases one's own understanding of balance and the relaxation qualities found within quieting both body and mind. It is an important part of games such as Firewood.

Breathing is relaxed, in through your nose, out through your mouth. Your eyes should be kept straight forward to utilize your peripheral vision. Hands should be close to your body, in front of you or placed lightly on your knees. As you lift up your front leg, keep your weight completely back on your rear leg, being careful not to lean forward. Take a short, natural step. As your foot comes down, gently touch the ground with the outside front of the foot

first, feeling the ground (weight still on rear leg). Once you are sure it is safe, slowly compress the rest of your foot. Next, carefully roll your weight forward, transferring the weight slowly to the front leg. Pick up the rear leg and repeat the process. Try to keep your head at the same level. Don't bob up and down. If you are doing it right you should be able to stop at any time in the stalk and not be off balance. The closer you get to your objective, the slower you go—until it looks like you are hardly moving at all.

Suggested Rules

1. Approach in as straight a line as possible. Don't sway side to side.
2. If an animal or person looks up, stop where you are.
3. Lift legs just high enough to get over any obstacles.
4. If possible, approach from downwind.
5. Don't change your type of stalk when close to an animal.
6. Slow your pace as you get closer.
7. Concentrate on breathing and balance.
8. Remain as calm as possible.
9. Don't concentrate too hard on what you are stalking. Look past it and clear your mind.

Stalking the Drum

This game, played with any number of participants, is aimed at both increasing one's balance as well as the use of other senses besides. Played either in a field, or for more advanced, in the forest, participants are blindfolded and lead off in different directions. Once everyone is situated, the runner of the game begins to beat a drum every so often. Those who are blindfolded must listen to and follow the beat of the drum. Once each participant makes it to the drum they are asked to remove their blindfold and step out of the way of the others.

Those who are blindfolded must listen to and follow the beat of the drum.

Suggested Rules

1. Participants must not try to move too fast; a medium-speed stalk works best.

2. It is best to have several judges watching out for the participants, especially when playing in the forest.

3. At first the drumbeater may move around a little, but should eventually become stationary.

4. Drumbeats should get further apart and softer as participants get closer.

Firewood

This game is best played outdoors with a multiple number of players—five to ten is best. Players sit in a large circle on the ground facing toward the center. Once all players are seated, one person in the circle puts on a blindfold. Two to four sticks are placed in front of the blindfolded player, who is the "fire-keeper." The fire-keeper must guard the wood as one anonymous person in the circle, the "fire-taker," tries to stalk toward the fire-keeper. The fire-taker attempts to quietly take one piece of firewood at a time. This game ends either when the fire-taker is touched, or when a stick is touched by the fire-keeper as the wood is being moved, or when all of the wood is taken.

The Firewood game is one of the best ways to teach the related skills of moving silently and listening closely.

Suggested Rules

1. The fire-keeper must sit with legs crossed, remaining seated on the ground at all times. Try to use your senses more than your hands.

2. Do not keep your hands on the firewood.

3. The fire-keeper should listen closely and try to hear the stalker.

4. The fire-taker must not grab the wood quickly. Take it as quietly as possible before the fire-keeper knows you are there.

5. Observers must be as quiet as possible. Talking or other sounds made by the observers can throw off the game.

The Rock Game

Best played with three or more participants, and often used when teaching tracking skills, this is another good game for honing the senses. Played indoors or out, participants are asked to stand in a circle about an arm's distance apart. Next they are asked to pick a small rock out of a bowl that is passed around the circle. It is best if there are slightly more rocks than participants. Once participants each have a rock, they are given a minute to memorize it. Participants should look at, feel, touch, and smell every detail of their rock. After a minute they are asked to place the rock back in the bowl.

Part 1. After shaking up the bowl of rocks, they are poured out onto the floor. Participants must walk forward, using their eyes, and find their rock as quickly as possible. After all the participants have found their rock, the rocks are placed back in the bowl.

Part 2. Next, each participant in the circle is blindfolded and told to get down on their hands and knees. When everyone is ready, the entire bowl of rocks is dumped in

Using every possible sense available, aside from their eyes, the players must try to find their rock.

the center of the circle. All at once, participants must carefully crawl forward to the pile. Using every possible sense available, aside from their eyes, they must try to find their rock.

Suggested Rules

1. At least one judge should be used to help keep the game safe and prevent any cheating. Depending on the age of participants, it can help to have each rock labeled with a number or other distinct sign. If labeled, signs should be either covered with tape or turned opposite side up during the visual portion of the game.

2. Blindfolds must be firmly placed over eyes. When crawling forward, participants must move slowly so as not to bump heads.

3. Once each participant believes they have found their rock, they must pick up the rock, carefully back away from the circle, and take off their blindfold.

4. If it is not their rock, a judge must place it back in the pile, allowing the others to continue.

5. It is up to those running the game to decide whether or not players are given a second chance.

Bibliography

There are a number of books that focus on Native American games. The following three, however, are the ones that we feel are the very best. Although they are not written for children, they will provide more than enough information for anyone wishing to know more about the wonderful, varied heritage of Native American sports.

Vennum, Thomas. *American Indian Lacrosse: Little Brother of War.* Washington D.C.: Smithsonian, 1994. A truly interesting history of the one modern sport that is thoroughly associated with its Native American roots. The book includes such things as imaginative accounts of how lacrosse was played in the past, the legends behind the game, and the many ways it was played and is still played by different Native nations.

Oxendine, Joseph B. *American Indian Sports Heritage.* Lincoln: University of Nebraska Press, 1995. The author is a member of the Lumbee Nation and his insider's view of American Indian sports is a thorough, highly readable study of the history and place of games in Native life. The book also devotes considerable space to the present-day place of sports among Native Americans, including profiles of such famous Indian athletes as Jim Thorpe, and to the ways Native Americans and the traditions of Native games contributed to the birth of modern team sports such as football.

Culin, Stewart. *Games of the American Indians.* Vol. 1, *Games of Chance.* Vol. 2, *Games of Skill.* Lincoln: University of Nebraska Press, 1992. First published in 1907 by the Bureau of American Ethnology, this incredible collection includes numerous illustrations, briefly told stories, and detailed information.

On the Sources of the Stories

Native American games were often played as a part of sacred and special occasions. We have tried to show our respect for those traditions in the way we have described these games and retold these stories and in our selection of the stories included.

Further, in this book we have chosen to tell only stories that are already known outside the original nations and have been previously published in order to avoid disclosing information about games that have special and sacred meanings to the Native nations who played them. Our desire is to share those things meant to be shared, not to expose things still meant to be kept private. Here is a list of some of the earliest printed versions of these stories.

"The Ball Game Between the Animals and the Birds"
Different versions of this story are widely told from the northeast to the southeast. It was published as an Akwesasne Mohawk tale in *Tewaarathon, Akwesasne's Story of Our National Game* (Native American Traveling College, 1978). The earliest recorded version of this story appears to be "How the Bat Got His Wings," found in *Myths of the Cherokee* by James Mooney (Washington, D.C.: Bureau of American Ethnology, 19th Annual Report, 1900).

"The Ball Players in the Sky"
Brown, Wallace. "The Strange Origin of Corn." *Journal of American Folklore*, no. 3, (1890).

"The Good Mind's Game"
Beauchamp, William M. *Iroquois Folk Lore: Gathered from the Six Nations of New York.* Port Washington, N.Y.: Kennikta Press, 1965.

"Kesitce: The Moccasin Game"
Matthews, Washington. "Navajo Gambling Songs." *The American Anthropologist* 11, (1898): 198.

"How Day and Night Came to Be"
Mooney, James. "The Jicarilla Genesis Myth." *The American Anthropologist* 11, (1889): 2.

"How the Two Brothers Followed the Hoop"
Dorsey, George A. *Traditions of the Caddo.* Washington, D.C.: Carnegie Institution of Washington, 1905.

"Nanabush and the Ducks"
Hoffman, Walter James. *The Menomini Indians.* Washington, D.C.: Bureau of American Ethnology, 14th Annual Report, 1896.

Index